RINGO'S ABBEY ROAD

ALEX CAIN
&
TERRY McCUSKER

ISBN 9781689720465

A *Ringo Starr And The Beatles Beat* book

©2020 Luddypool Books

Web

www.beatlesbeat.com

Email

info@beatlesbeat.com

Facebook

www.facebook.com/ringostarrandthebeatlesbeat

Twitter

@beatlesbeatbook

Instagram

beatlesbeatbook

Alex dedicates this book to his wonderful wife Joanne for her continuing help and support, and to Daniel, Benjamin, and Joseph for yet again subjecting them to constant Beatles music. At least this time around it was only a single LP rather than a double.

Terry dedicates this book to Tom and Moll, for their endless patience.

CONTENTS

PART ONE

OVERVIEW

About The Authors

Alex was born in Liverpool, as the Beatles' latest single *Eleanor Rigby/Yellow Submarine* sat atop the charts. A drummer for many years, he has enjoyed a career in TV sound, across numerous productions for BBC, ITV, C4 and independents. He lives in Liverpool, works in Liverpool, and of course, supports Everton.

Within three years of seeing the Beatles at the Cavern, Terry was himself playing the sweat-clubs of Germany and elsewhere. Working as a freelancer he has played all over Europe, America and the Middle East with many varied bands and artists on stage, screen or radio. Still in demand, he can be seen doing anything from powering along a ten-piece, or merely standing up playing his cocktail kit with a trio in his local pub.

Preface

Since *Ringo Starr And The Beatles Beat* was first published, we received many requests to expand upon the chapters dealing with specific albums. Marking the fiftieth anniversary of the release of *The Beatles*, commonly referred to as the *White Album*, *Ringo's White Album* was published. The fiftieth anniversary of *Abbey Road* again lends us the opportunity to explore Ringo's contribution to a standalone Beatles LP.

As with *Ringo Starr And The Beatles Beat and Ringo's White Album*, the aim has been to highlight Ringo's role and his band-mate's use of percussion, and how they both shaped the overall sound of the LP. We hope die-hard and casual fans (including drummers and non-drummers) enjoy the book, and are able to dig deeper into the incredible music on Abbey Road.

Throughout their career, the Beatles often recorded songs which were destined for release as stand-alone singles at the same time as album tracks. The *I Feel Fine / She's A Woman* single was recorded during the *Beatles For Sale* sessions, the *Hey Jude / Revolution* single during *White Album* sessions, and so on. As they were part of the same timeframe within sessions that bore fruit on *Abbey Road*, we have included and expanded upon the *Ballad Of John And Yoko* and *Old Brown Shoe* single.

Due to the large number of songs on the *White Album, Ringo's White Album* was published in two separate editions - Standard and Deluxe, the latter containing the *White Album* drum and percussion scores. *Ringo's Abbey Road* is only available in one edition, and contains the complete drum and percussion scores, making it the stand-alone one-stop shop for Ringo's work on the LP.

While it's nigh-on impossible to single out a Beatles LP to highlight Ringo's contribution to the Beatles' musical landscape, *Abbey Road* must come close. Now at ease with his new Ludwig Hollywood drum kit which debuted on the *White Album*, his artistry throughout *Abbey Road* arguably hit a peak. From the delicate strokes on his floor tom and cymbals during *Sun King*, to the 'restrained one moment, forceful the next' tom work of *Something and* the 'swampy' rhythms of *Come Together,* we are hearing Ringo at his very best, a lesson in how to play either with economy or with fierce abandon, yet always demonstrating empathy for the moment. Truly, Ringo was the finest drummer the Beatles could have wished for.

The Beatles '69

"It doesn't matter what we go through as individuals on the bullshit level. When it gets to the music, you can see that it's really cool, and we had all put in 1,000 percent." **Ringo Starr** [1]

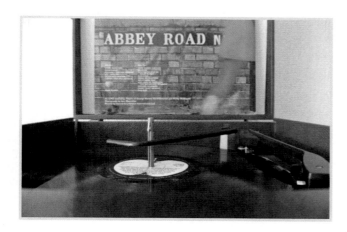

With the *White Album* release finally behind them, Paul McCartney once again proved to be the driving force behind future projects. Boosted by the group's joyful experience of performing before an audience during the *Hey Jude* promo film recording, Paul's suggestion was a return to live performances. At one stage the Roundhouse was reportedly booked for a TV special, with free tickets offered through the *Beatles Book Monthly* magazine. However this scheme faltered, with inertia and disinterest within the band to blame.

A new project was floated - a film to document rehearsals for forthcoming live performances. Filming of group rehearsals began on January 2nd 1969 at Twickenham Studios, with Michael Lindsay Hogg directing. However, the cold, sterile atmosphere coupled with the open nature of the soundstage proved detrimental to the sound and bonhomie of the band. Beatles' recording sessions usually took place late in the day, continuing until the early hours of the following morning, the mood here not helped by the early morning call times commonplace within the film industry. By January 10th, George had had enough, and quit the band during a particularly tense session with the classic line "See you 'round the clubs" ringing around the cavernous studio.

Less than a week later, George agreed to return, on the proviso any notion of live performances was shelved. It was agreed filming would continue at the fledgling Apple Studios, the focus now to document the processes involved in producing the next Beatles record. Matters improved, with sessions becoming productive - the highlight proving to be the Beatles' last live performance famously taking place on the roof of their Savile Row HQ.

Many of the songs destined for *Abbey Road* were demoed and rehearsed during filming, indeed sessions took place just 3 weeks after the Let It Be filming was completed. It is unclear if the recording of the backing track of *I Want You (She's So Heavy)* was destined for the *Let It Be* project or the new LP, but further sessions were curtailed due to Ringo's commitments to his role in the *Magic Christian*. This however didn't stop Lennon cajoling McCartney into recording the *Ballad Of John And Yoko* without Ringo and George, the B-Side recording of George's *Old Brown Shoe* apparently also sans Ringo due to his filming schedule.

While the tone of the *Abbey Road* sessions was cordial and the results fruitful, the recordings were not without drama. John Lennon and Yoko Ono had been involved in a motor accident whilst visiting relatives in Scotland, and as a result Lennon was absent from initial sessions for the album. He does not therefore feature on three tracks - *Maxwell's Silver Hammer, Here Comes The Sun, and Golden Slumbers*.[2] Further friction was added by the installation of a bed in the studio, from which Yoko could recuperate from her injuries - and tellingly, cast her eye over proceedings. With her bed-ridden presence heightening tensions, Yoko did herself no favours by quietly creeping from her bed to help herself to Harrison's McVitie's digestive biscuits. George was not amused.

Traditional views of the recording of *Abbey Road* offer a tale of the group enlisting George Martin, who on his terms would produce in a manner befitting their pre-*White Album* work, with disciplined, workmanlike sessions the order of the day. This was to be their final album - a "last hurrah!" befitting their illustrious past. However, further group meetings (which were fortunately recorded for the benefit of absent members) indicate a willingness, especially and unusually by Lennon, for the group to continue as a recording entity. A matter of weeks later however, on September 20th 1969, John Lennon dropped the bombshell - "I want a divorce".

Although ultimately released prior to *Let It Be*, *Abbey Road* sees The Beatles exiting on a high - alongside Geoff Emerick's skilful handling of the new transistor technology, George Martin's production adds gloss to the incredible musicianship and songwriting talent at their disposal - a fitting epitaph when placed against the "cardboard tombstone"[3] of *Let It Be*.

Recorded by THE BEATLES on Apple Records
SOMETHING
Words and Music by GEORGE HARRISON

BEATLES

ABBEY ROAD

75843
HARRISONGS MUSIC, INC./HARRISONGS MUSIC LTD.

3/6
$1.00

PART TWO

HOW TO USE THIS BOOK

Content

Technicalities

Timings relative to the music are indicated beneath bars, allowing the reader to accurately follow the description or notation of the songs. Regarding notation, as Ringo is a drummer with such a great amount of 'feel', it is pertinent to note it is sometimes impossible to transcribe the subtle nuances of his playing. Ringo played ever so slightly *behind* the beat, he would often strike the drum skins milliseconds either side of the natural beat (as indeed 99% of drummers do), and as such this is impossible to accurately represent in notation form. However (occasionally using grace notes) we have attempted to remedy this, presenting Ringo's patterns as accurately as possible. Each song's engineer is listed, as their contribution had a bearing upon the overall sound that was captured on tape.

Time Signatures

The time signature (or *meter*) of each song is stated below the title of each song description, for example:

Come Together

Time Signature – 4/4

Where appropriate, and to unclutter bars, we have occasionally removed rests. Timing will still be obvious due to notes of other instruments occurring where rests have been removed.

Data

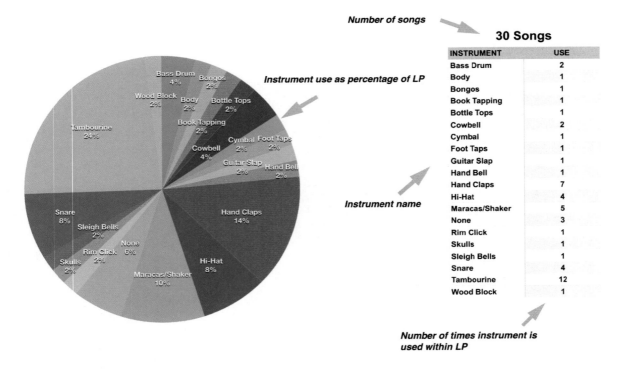

Number of songs

30 Songs

Instrument use as percentage of LP

Instrument name

INSTRUMENT	USE
Bass Drum	2
Body	1
Bongos	1
Book Tapping	1
Bottle Tops	1
Cowbell	2
Cymbal	1
Foot Taps	1
Guitar Slap	1
Hand Bell	1
Hand Claps	7
Hi-Hat	4
Maracas/Shaker	5
None	3
Rim Click	1
Skulls	1
Sleigh Bells	1
Snare	4
Tambourine	12
Wood Block	1

Number of times instrument is used within LP

Data charts display the percussion instruments used by the Beatles on *Abbey Road*. Where the only percussion instruments present are drums (eg *Oh! Darling*), we have displayed this as 'Drums (No Percussion)'. On the rare occasions there are no drums or percussion, we have displayed this as 'No Drums/Percussion'. Where songs have instruments that make-up a set of drums and are played in isolation or form the dominant feature, we have treated them as individual, separate instruments.

Terminology

Regarding *drumming* and *recording* terminology, we have assumed most readers have a basic understanding of such matters. However, we have attempted to simplify matters as much as possible, rather than alienate (and bore) readers who have little technical knowledge of the subject. The Beatles often referred to 'bridge' sections of songs as 'middle 8's', regardless of how many bars are actually contained in the bridge. We refer to these passages as either 'bridges' or 'middle 8's'. On a slightly pedantic note, we refer to the British term 'bass drum', rather than the more modern term 'kick drum'.

The Scores

With these listening choices in mind, the scores (both the excerpts within the text and the complete scores) are based upon the original *Abbey Road* mix. There may be occasional references to the 2019 remix, but the original mix is still considered the standard *Abbey Road* mix of the Beatles' catalogue. We have taken our song start and end timings from the perspective of a drummer, not a mastering engineer marking tracks for a CD or streaming.

Listening Sources

Our initial points of reference were the original mix via a vinyl UK first pressing, plus the 44.1 kHz / 24 bit files on the Apple USB stick.

We delayed publication to assess the 50th Anniversary remix via the 96/24 hi-res blu-ray, cd, and vinyl. The remix, undertaken by Giles Martin and Sam Okell at Abbey Road, enhances Ringo's contribution to *Abbey Road,* his drums appearing more prominent, with the placement and clarity of overdubs especially benefitting. The box set *Sessions* also reveal the songs as works in progress, with the importance of drum

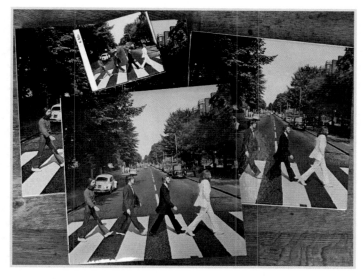

overdubs to the finished product. To the uninitiated, the differences between a remix and a remaster can be confusing. Essentially a remix involves revisiting the original master tapes and altering the relationships between the different tracks as originally mixed. So, a vocal track that was originally panned to the left channel may be 'centred' by being placed in both the left and right channels, or a drum overdub may be moved and possibly increased or decreased in level. A remaster simply leaves the original mix as is, running the master tape through a series of filters, cleaning-up the signal in the process. Other changes to the sound of the master tape may be applied, such as equalisation (EQ) and compression, but as a remaster only deals with one (mono) or two (stereo) tracks, no changes are made between the original individual tracks.

We were also fortunate to listen to the Beatles *Rock Band* mix stems - while not truly indicative of the recording process, it is possible to hear the drums and percussion in isolation - a fantastic resource when transcribing Ringo's drum parts.

A Short Guide To Drum Notation

This book is not intended to be a drum tutor – indeed the subtleties and nuances of Ringo's instinctive drumming make it virtually impossible to transcribe his playing accurately. Additionally, a great deal of the (sometimes overdubbed) percussion is buried deep in the mix and is difficult to hear, let alone commit to bars of drum notation. As a result, our transcriptions are entirely our own interpretation of what we are able to hear.

As there is no international standard of drum notation, we are bound by the notation software, namely Musescore. North American readers may notice very slight variations, especially open-hi-hat notation, however a glance at this chapter will soon rectify matters and will not hamper your reading of the scores.

Time Signatures

4/4 is the most used time signature (or meter) in Western music – indeed, for this reason, it is referred to as 'common time'. The bottom number tells you the value of the note, and the top number tells you how many of those there are in the bar. Taking that into account, in the bars below we can see that a bar indicating 2/4 tells us that we should count twice per bar: 1, 2.... etc. With a bar of 3/4 we count 1,2,3.... a bar of 4/4 we count 1,2,3,4...and so on.

You may be forgiven for thinking that all Beatles songs are in this simple 4/4 time, because they are all so easy to sing along to. However, Lennon, McCartney, and Harrison were true wordsmiths, and often found themselves in the position of having to make the music 'fit' the words. Consequently, many *Abbey Road* songs have multiple time signatures within a few bars of each other – *Here Comes The Sun* a prime example. It's testament to Ringo's drumming skills that the listener is largely unaware of such changes in meter.

Drum Notation

In the following first bar we have one whole note, indicating that single note lasts for the duration of the bar – we should therefore count '4' for the length of the bar. The second bar shows that whole note halved, indicating two notes are being played: so we should count '2' for each half note. The third bar contains four 1/4 notes, count '1' for each note, and so on..... The final bar contains 16th notes - we should therefore quickly count 16 times the length of time we counted the whole note of the first bar.

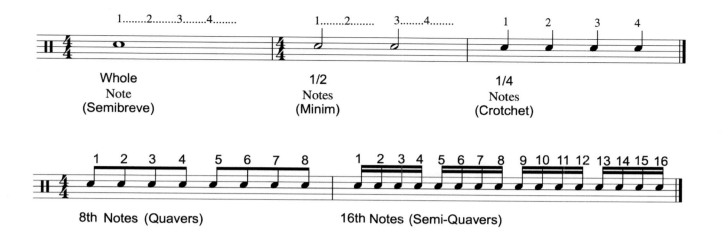

Whole Note (Semibreve)
1/2 Notes (Minim)
1/4 Notes (Crotchet)

8th Notes (Quavers)
16th Notes (Semi-Quavers)

So, for the purposes of our notation, the following bar displays the most common 1/8th note hi-hat pattern. As these quavers are the lowest notes of value, we can easily deduce where the bass and snare drums are struck.

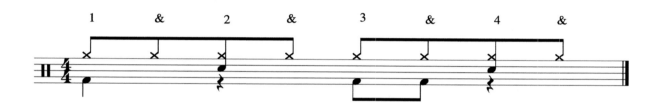

Rests

As we have seen, a note indicates a beat of specific length, conversely, a rest is merely a silence of a certain length. Where no notes are played, rests take their place. However, for the purposes of simplicity (and avoiding the bars looking as if we have swatted a fly upon them), we have removed some rests where their place is indicated by a note or rest on another line. Looking at the previous bar, we are able to accurately place the bass drum and snare without using rests.

Here we have illustrated the commonly used rests. We can see how they relate to each other within bars, and also (in the second example) how they relate to other notes.

Whole note rest
1/2 note rest
1/4 note rest
1/8 note rest
1/16 note rest
1/32 note rest

'Dotted' Notes

To fully appreciate Ringo's famed drumming 'feel', it is crucial to understand the role of 'dotted' notes.

In the diagram below we can see that the dot in the first note increases the duration of that note by half of its original value.

and so forth......

Looking at the notation below, we can see how the bass drum has a 'dotted' note, creating the impression of a longer passage of time, and therefore inserting 'feel', or a human element to the song. Of course, there are still the same number of notes available within each bar.......

Without this 'dotted' note, the drum pattern would appear slightly rigid or 'robotic'.

Notation Articulations

Occasionally we have used 'articulations' to emphasise aspects of Ringo's drumming that are difficult to translate to bars of notation.

Accents

In the following bars, with the use of accents (the symbol **>**), we can see Ringo placing emphasis on the snare beats by accenting the 5th and13th notes of the tambourine.

Crescendo and Fade

The symbol ⟍ beneath a bar denotes a passage gradually becoming louder across its denoted length, usually associated with an instrument being brought into the mix by the engineer.

Conversely, a fade is denoted by the symbol ⟍

Repeats

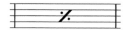

As an aid to those readers who are unfamiliar with drum notation, we have not utilised bar repeats (symbol above) as the songs (and use of percussion within) are easier to follow fully notated. In short, without repeats one can easily see and appreciate the layout of percussion alongside the drum track.

Drum Notation Key

By the time of the *Abbey Road* sessions, Ringo was now permanently playing his 5-piece Ludwig Hollywood kit.

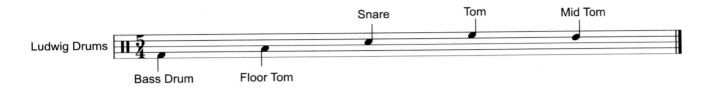

Cymbal Notation Key

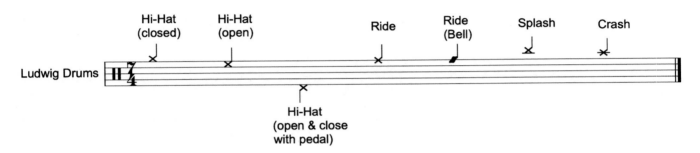

Perhaps due to having a limited (but for the day perfectly adequate) set-up, Ringo was inventive with his use of cymbals. A typical set-up of the day included hi-hats, ride, and crash cymbals. As it has proven troublesome to accurately document the type of cymbals Ringo used, we have found it difficult to translate exactly what type of cymbals he was playing with any degree of certainty. We do however know Ringo used the same Zildjian hi-hats throughout the Beatles' recording career, but alas this doesn't help us a great deal, as we know when he is playing hi-hats – after all, a pair of hi-hats are 'a pair of hi-hats'. The same cannot be said for differentiating between a crash and a crash/ride cymbal.

One fact we *can* be sure of, is on *Abbey Road* Ringo extensively used a sizzle cymbal. A sizzle cymbal has a series of rivets positioned within holes around the cymbal edge, which unsurprisingly lends a 'sizzle' effect when struck. It seems Ringo used his sizzle either as a crash or ride cymbal, to fill the air with a sound he was unable to obtain from his other cymbals. For simplicity, we have notated this use as either 'ride' or 'crash' cymbals. Ringo's sizzle cymbal can clearly be heard on the bridges between verse and chorus of *Maxwell's Silver Hammer*.

A feature of Ringo's early drumming is the use of (partially) open or 'swishy' hi-hats. To a lesser extent he was still employing the technique in 1969. Again, this is virtually impossible to transcribe, as drum notation tells us hi-hats are either (fully) open or closed. Due to this, when Ringo employs his famous open hi-hats, we treat them as being closed. A similar arrangement has been employed with his cymbal work, on tracks such as *I Want You (She's So Heavy)*, we have utilised accents to highlight his crash/ride technique. Additionally, Ringo's use of his ride cymbal bell has been noted on this track.

When placed alongside diagrams of his drum kit, we can see how Ringo's playing is transcribed. Due to damping, it is occasionally difficult to distinguish between the toms.

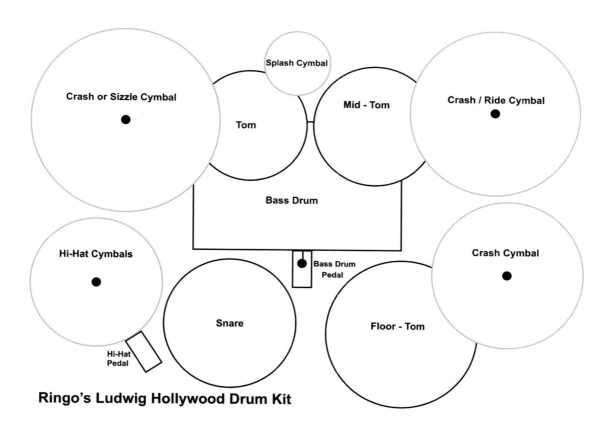

Ringo's Ludwig Hollywood Drum Kit

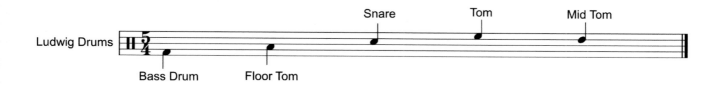

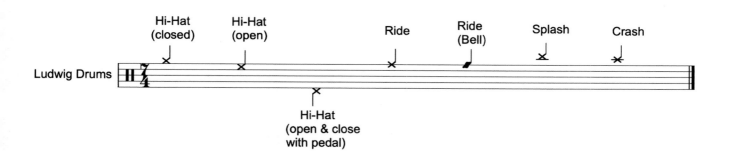

PART THREE

THE STUDIO ENVIRONMENT

The Beatles' Studio Practices

During their early studio career, the Beatles would rehearse a song as a group, and when happy with the results, would proceed to make recordings. As the Beatles' songwriting and use of the studio expanded, the framework of songs would be brought to the studio, where they would be further developed with the guiding hand of George Martin. As a result, the group performed less as a single unit. By the time of *Magical Mystery Tour* in late 1967, this practice had reached a peak. Basic recordings were routinely made with drums, guitar and/or piano, and perhaps a guide vocal. Bass guitar and other embellishments (percussive, orchestral, or vocal etc.) would then be added to the original take.

The fractured nature of the *White Album* recordings led to the return of a 'group' ethos during the *Get Back/Let It Be* sessions, with recordings eschewing overdubs as much as possible. With many of the *Abbey Road* songs being demoed and rehearsed during these sessions, recording of Abbey Road was efficient and rapid. Many tracks were indeed remade from sessions earlier in the year, *Something* a case in point, while others were reconstructed (*I Want You (She's So Heavy)*), or resurrected from the *White Album* Esher Demos (*Polythene Pam, Mean Mr. Mustard*). Overdubs were largely percussive, and employed where necessary to bolster the rhythmic nature of the songs. When allied to the technological advances in the studio, the end result was an album bristling with musicianship.

Abbey Road Producers And Engineers

George Martin

Born in 1926, Sir George is the most successful British record producer, and is widely credited as the 'Fifth Beatle'. However, it's fair to say that it was his close relationship with his engineers that shaped the Beatles' sound, and guided them through their musical development. Classically trained on piano and oboe, George Martin wore his Producer's hat superbly, taking on the mantle of mentor rather than an all-out father-figure. The ill-feeling that pervaded the *White Album* sessions proved to be the tipping point for Martin, and he decided to take a break from proceedings. Martin returned for the ill-fated *Get Back* sessions, and was coaxed back for the group's final album, *Abbey Road*, as long as the sessions were on his terms, recording in the manner of days gone by. Knighted in 1996, Sir George passed away in 2016.

Engineers

The Beatles benefited greatly from the 'in-house' talent at their disposal. New, young engineers had a strict but rapid career progression at Abbey Road. Most started work in the Tape Library, where they became familiar with tape formats, labelling protocol, etc, the perfect education for preparing for life as the next step-up – into the studio environment as assistant engineer. Sometimes referred to as 2nd engineer, this job would involve operating the tape machines, labelling, compiling album tapes from individual masters, and making sure recordings were actually made to tape. Assistants were more or less tied to their chair in front of the tape machine – under no circumstances were they allowed to touch the mixing console, microphones or other studio ephemera.

Progression would then be made outside of the recording studio environment to the post of mastering engineer (or cutter), whose duties involved the transfer of the completed, mixed tapes to disc. 'Cutting' was an extremely important and responsible job, if a little solitary.

Back into the studio, next on the ladder was the position of (balance) engineer, whose responsibilities would (unsurprisingly) include balancing the recordings through the mixing console before they were committed to tape. Engineers would also be responsible for duties such as microphone placement, adding of compression and equalisation, and contributing to the final mixes.

Abbey Road LP - Principal Engineers

Geoff Emerick

Born in London in 1946, Geoff Emerick arguably added the greatest creative input to the Beatles' sound. Possessing a love of recorded sound, with the help of his school careers officer Geoff secured an interview with EMI at Abbey Road. Within weeks he was in place at Abbey Road, and present at the Beatles' first recording session. In 1966 he was promoted to engineer, and whilst working on the *Revolver* sessions, his impact was immediate.

Emerick worked on most of the Beatles' sessions until, during the *White Album* recordings, effectively 'burned-out', he couldn't take any more of the acrimony and bitterness that pervaded and refused to work with the group. He was however persuaded to return as engineer for the *Abbey Road* recordings, completing the team for one 'last hurrah'. *Abbey Road* was very nearly named after Geoff's penchant for the *Everest* brand of cigarettes. Particularly enamoured of Paul McCartney's dedication to his art, Geoff would engineer many of his albums from the 1970's and 80's, most notably *Band On The Run*, for which (along with *Abbey Road* and *Sgt. Pepper*) he was awarded a Grammy for *Best Engineered Recording – Non Classical*. Geoff passed away in October 2018.

Alan Parsons

Alan first came to prominence as an assistant engineer on *Abbey Road* sessions, and is perhaps best known for his work on Pink Floyd's *Dark Side Of The Moon,* plus his *Alan Parsons Project* albums.

John Kurlander

At the recommendation of George Martin and Geoff Emerick, John assisted *Abbey Road* sessions, and subsequently engineered solo Beatles projects. He has forged a successful engineering and producing career, specialising in orchestral work, most notably the *Lord Of The Rings* trilogy scores.

The New Sonic Texture

"The new sonic texture actually suited the music on the album—softer and rounder. It's subtle, but I'm convinced the sound of that new console and tape machine overtly influenced the performance and the music." **Geoff Emerick** [4]

(Left - Abbey Road's surviving TG 12345 mixing desk)

By the late 1960's, EMI Studios had a reputation of being 'behind the curve' of the latest technological developments. With Trident Studios possessing the U.K.'s first 8-track recorder, the Beatles were seduced by the charms of the Sheffield brothers' newly opened establishment, recording *White Album* tracks plus the monster hit *Hey Jude* there in 1968. Little did they know EMI had their own 8-track, which was undergoing rigorous testing before deployment. In true Beatle fashion, the machine was soon liberated and put to work by the impatient George Harrison, forsaking the engineers cautionary stance. While seemingly draconian, with costly studio down-time due to mechanical gremlins best avoided, such a diktat was understandable.

With the 'white heat'[5] of technological advances in tow, the EMI boffins were already working on a new development - the replacement of the trusty REDD valve console with a transistor based mixing desk. Simply put, valves (vacuum tubes) are renowned for a 'warmer' sound, against the 'cleaner' sound created by transistors. Transistors are less prone to failure than valves, and offer greater flexibility and ease of use. Compared to the 8 inputs and four outputs of the REDD, the transistor powered TG 12345 increased the number of inputs to 24, outputting to 8 tracks - a massive increase in the engineer's armoury. Each channel had its own compressor/limiter, with equalisation on each channel group, with later versions placing the eq on each channel.

While the TG12345 desk provided a smoother, more polished sound than earlier Beatles recordings, Geoff Emerick found he was unable to recreate the gritty compression of the valve desks -

"With the TG console, in no way could I re-create the same bass drum, snare drum, or guitar sounds that I'd been able to get on the REDD valve consoles," he recalled. "I'd only used the REDD valve consoles (and tape machines) on Beatles sessions up to that point, and I think that the tubes played a big part in those sounds. I found that the transistors clipped everything, they wouldn't let any low end distortion go through." [6]

Donated to a local school in the mid 1970's, the TG12345 desk was rescued from a skip, and now resides in a private collection.

Ringo's Abbey Road Drums

Switching from his Ludwig Super Classic kit mid-way through the *White Album* sessions, 1969 saw Ringo exclusively playing his new Ludwig Hollywood drums. Freed from the restraints of working with just two tom-toms, the addition of a 12" x 8" tom expanded and enhanced Ringo's distinctive drumming style. Songs such as *Something* and *Polythene Pam* saw his rhythmic tom work brought to the fore, adding a new dimension to the Beatles' sound. Ringo initially placed his toms on a stand (as illustrated by Gary Astridge's replica below), however by the time of *Abbey Road*, he had chosen to mount his toms on the bass drum.

Ringo's Ludwig Hollywood Drums

Maple finish
12" x 8" Tom
13" x 9" Tom
16" x 16" Tom
22" x 14" Bass Drum

Ludwig Jazz Festival Snare Drum

Oyster Black Pearl Finish
Wooden shell
14" x 5.5"

Despite possessing a new set of drums, Ringo continued to use his trusty Ludwig Jazz Festival snare. Date stamped 18 April 1963, Ringo's Jazz Festival was purchased from Drum City in London with his first Ludwig kit – the Downbeat. The Downbeat was usually supplied with the smaller Downbeat Piccolo snare, the larger metal shelled Supraphonic being supplied with the Super Classic set. This makes Ringo's 5.5" Jazz Festival all the rarer – Ringo's drum curator Gary Astridge knows of only four other 1963 Jazz Festivals of this specification. It is likely they were a special-order item, although quite why Ringo's was shipped to England remains a mystery. A testament to the dependability and signature sound of Ringo's Jazz Festival, he played it on the Beatles recorded output from late 1963 to the group's demise.

Pictured above right: The limited edition Starr Festival snare - a replica in every detail of Ringo's iconic Jazz Festival [7]

Ringo's Cymbals

Zildjian Crash/Ride – 18"
Zildjian 'A' Hi-Hats – 15"
Zyn or Super Zyn Sizzle Cymbal – 20"
Crash – 16"
Splash Cymbal

Ringo favoured a sizzle cymbal, a type of cymbal that features rivets attached through holes drilled into the cymbal, giving the cymbal a long "sizzle" sounding decay. This is incredibly useful when the intention is to bridge passages of music, or the fading finale of a song. A sizzle cymbal is especially versatile, (as is the case with all cymbals) as the resulting effect is dependent upon the strength with which the cymbal is struck. Ringo's sizzle cymbal is especially prominent on *Abbey Road*, featuring strongly between the verse/chorus transitions of *Maxwell's Silver Hammer*.

Featured during *Here Comes The Sun* (prominent at [0.59]) is a splash cymbal - a small diameter cymbal that provides a punchier, shorter decay than the more common size cymbals.

Ringo has always stated he used a pair of Zildjian 'A' hi-hats with the Beatles, and photos appear to back-up his statement.[8] He also favoured a Zildjian Crash/Ride, and with the acquisition of his Hollywood set, added a further crash cymbal.

Ringo's Bongos

Ringo employed bongos extensively throughout his Beatles career, first a set that came with his Mahogany Duroplastic Premier drums, then latterly a set of Ludwig that were used on *Abbey Road*. Listen out for bongos on *Sun King*.

Left: Ludwig bongos identical to those owned by Ringo.

Recording Ringo's Drums

"I love drums, and I wanted them to have more impact" **Geoff Emerick** [9]

The EMI engineers worked hard over the years to improve Ringo's drum sound. As the Beatles progressively pushed back boundaries, so would the engineering team. EMI's strict rules on recording determined the sound of the Beatles' early recordings and were ruthlessly enforced.

In the early 1960's, Rock'n'Roll was still the new kid on the block, with classical recordings making up the bulk of Abbey Road's output. The physical layout, and manner in which orchestras performed dictated how the recording engineers approached their task, with regimented microphone placement the order of the day.

Engineers would have to take into account the dynamic range of classical music, quiet passages of music often being followed by incredibly loud ones. A band such as the Beatles however, presented a different challenge. Recording a song with such power as possessed by *Twist And Shout* would have placed stresses upon the microphones of the day, especially when placed closely to drums and amplifiers, and would have been seen as potentially damaging to the equipment. The 'powers that be' certainly weren't ready to allow four scruffs from the provinces any close contact with their sensitive equipment. As a result, the microphones were positioned at what was considered a 'safe distance' from the drums – laughable by the close-miking techniques in use by the end of the Beatles career.

The engineering team would incrementally experiment with the recording of Ringo's drums. On early Beatles' recordings, Ringo's drums were treated to a bass drum microphone (positioned a regulatory 2 feet away), with an overhead microphone a foot or so above his head, hoping to capture the other drums and cymbals as best they could. By the time of *Sgt. Pepper*, the bass drum microphone was positioned right up against the drum head, and was joined not only by one overhead, (this time positioned more forward and closer), but also another a couple of inches above the floor tom, one below the mounted tom, and finally one positioned above the snare and hi-hats. The bottom heads of the toms were also occasionally removed, further reducing the 'ring' of the drum, and therefore requiring less damping of the top skin.

To deal with the close proximity of the microphone placement, compressors were utilised – devices which would control the level of the audio signal by reducing the dynamic range (the difference between the loudest and quietest passages) of the audio signal from the microphones. Prior to *Abbey Road*, EMI employed Fairchild compressors on Ringo's drums, however with the installation of the new solid state TG12345 console, limiters were pre-installed on each input channel. Despite this change in approach, Geoff Emerick was able to reproduce the distinctive sound everyone wanted to emulate -

"This was the first time I was able to record his kit in stereo because we were using eight-track instead of four-track. Because of this, I had more mic inputs, so I could mic from underneath the toms, place more mics around the kit - the sound of his drums were finally captured in full. I think when he heard this, he kind of perked up and played more forcefully on the toms, and with more creativity." [10]

Damping Ringo's Drums

"He would always lay a soft pack of cigarettes on the snare drum. We tried something else once and it didn't work. Sometimes we used tea towels over the toms and snare to get a deader sound." **Geoff Emerick** [11]

Controlling the 'open' sound of an acoustic drum kit is always a challenge, more so in the 1960's studio environment. Since the *Beatles For Sale* album sessions in 1964, EMI's engineers had occasionally draped Ringo's drums with tea towels in an attempt to deaden the lively sound, seeking to match the sound of his drums to the dynamics of particular songs. With specific reference to *Abbey Road*, there's no greater example of damping Ringo's drums than *Come Together*.

By the time of *Abbey Road*, this had become standard practice – indeed it had been adopted industry wide. The days of the lively, open drum sound were numbered. When coupled with multiple miking of individual drums and cymbals, deadening of the drums allowed greater control of the drum kit overall, with reverb added later to compensate for too 'dry' a sound. By now, the front drum head was routinely removed, allowing microphone placement not only closer to the bass drum, but inside it. A blanket or clothing (a jumper) was placed inside to further deaden the sound, providing a solid 'thwack' rather than the 'booming', 'ringing' sound resulting from the drum having two heads fitted. This would give the engineers greater control of the sound of the bass drum through compression and equalisation.

Additionally, *Abbey Road* saw calf skin heads fitted to Ringo's Hollywood drums. The Beatles had been through a 'natural sound' phase, where instruments were stripped of paint to apparently lend an organic sound to recordings. What may appear to have been a fad does have merits, with calf skin heads giving a warm, rounded sound, indeed the signature sound of Ringo's work on *Abbey Road*.

Above: Gary Astridge's replica of Ringo's Ludwig Hollywood drum set.

THE LUDWIG HOLLYWOOD

...the latest in "Twin" tom tom design

Ludwig's advance design and creative imagination has developed the ideal outfit for today's modern "Rock" drummer. The HOLLYWOOD features the new all-angle retracting double tom holder that provides complete angle and height adjustment and allows use of mixed tom tom sizes. The popular Supra-Phonic 400 all-metal snare drum and the famous 201 Speed King pedal are standard. Three different tom tom sizes (8" x 12", 9" x 13", 16" x 16") provide a wide variety of tonal changes and modern effects.

No. 983-1PC—HOLLYWOOD OUTFIT. Choice of pearl finish, chrome, **WITHOUT CYMBALS** $568.00

Recommended PAISTE-Formula 602 CYMBALS for HOLLYWOOD OUTFIT

2 No. 714HH—14" Matched for Hi-Hat @ $31.50 each.........................$ 63.00
1 No. 718TC—18" Thin Crash.................. 47.00
1 No. 720MR—20" Medium Ride.............. 58.00
　TOTAL VALUE, Cymbals $168.00

No. 226—Set of 4 PAISTE-Formula 602 **CYMBALS,** as above, special price .$160.00

No. 983-1PCX—HOLLYWOOD OUTFIT. Choice of pearl finish, **WITH PAISTE CYMBALS** listed above, special combination price...............$728.00

Outfit includes:

		Chrome
1	No. 400—5" x 14" All-Metal Snare.............................	$ 92.50
1	No. 922PC—14" x 22" Bass Drum, pearl................	138.50
1	No. 942PC—8" x 12" Tom Tom, pearl....................	71.00
1	No. 944PC—9" x 13" Tom Tom, pearl	73.00
1	No. 950PC—16" x 16" Tom Tom, pearl...................	107.00
1	No. 781-1—Retracting Double Tom Tom Holder........	20.00
1	No. 1123-1—Hi-Hat Pedal Stand..........................	24.00
1	No. 1363—Flat Base Snare Drum Stand...................	14.00
2	No. 1400—Floor Stand Cymbal Holder....................	24.00
1	No. 201—Speed King Pedal.................................	25.00
1 pr.	No. 1305C—Folding Spurs..............................	7.00
1 pr.	No. 193—Wire Brushes.................................	2.50
1 pr.	No. 8A—Orchestra Model Sticks.......................	1.50
	TOTAL VALUE, Drums and Accessories.............	$600.00

Sparkling Gold Pearl Illustrated

8

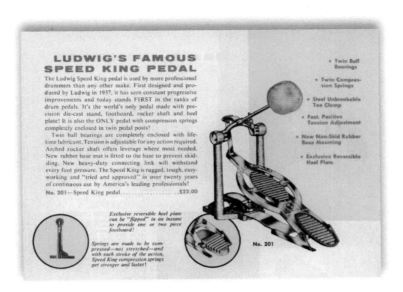

LUDWIG'S FAMOUS SPEED KING PEDAL

The Ludwig Speed King pedal is used by more professional drummers than any other make. First designed and produced by Ludwig in 1937, it has seen constant progressive improvements and today stands FIRST in the ranks of drum pedals. It's the world's only pedal made with precision die-cast stand, footboard, rocker shaft and heel plate! It is also the ONLY pedal with compression springs completely enclosed in twin pedal posts!

Twin ball bearings are completely enclosed with lifetime lubricant. Tension is adjustable for any action required. Arched rocker shaft offers leverage where most needed. New rubber base mat is fitted to the base to prevent skidding. New heavy-duty connecting link will withstand every foot pressure. The Speed King is rugged, tough, easy-working and "tried and approved" in over twenty years of continuous use by America's leading professionals!

No. 201—Speed King pedal.......................$22.00

- Twin Ball Bearings
- Twin Compression Springs
- Steel Unbreakable Toe Clamp
- Fast, Positive Tension Adjustment
- New Non-Skid Rubber Base Mounting
- Exclusive Reversible Heel Plate

Exclusive reversible heel plate can be "flipped" in an instant to provide one or two piece footboard!

Springs are made to be compressed—not stretched—and with each stroke of the action, Speed King compression springs get stronger and faster!

No. 201

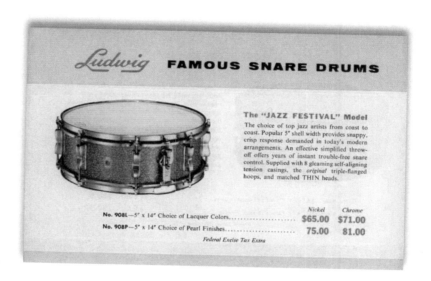

Ludwig FAMOUS SNARE DRUMS

The "JAZZ FESTIVAL" Model

The choice of top jazz artists from coast to coast. Popular 5" shell width provides snappy, crisp response demanded in today's modern arrangements. An effective simplified throw-off offers years of instant trouble-free snare control. Supplied with 8 gleaming self-aligning tension casings, the *original* triple-flanged hoops, and matched THIN heads.

	Nickel	Chrome
No. 908L—5" x 14" Choice of Lacquer Colors.....................	$65.00	$71.00
No. 908P—5" x 14" Choice of Pearl Finishes.....................	75.00	81.00

Federal Excise Tax Extra

LUDWIG *tunable bongos*

Ludwig professional model tunable bongos are supplied with 6" and 8" head diameters and 5½" shell depth. Sturdy laminated reinforced shells are built for extreme high tension required for authentic bongo sound. Conventional key tuning provides instant head tensioning with the least amount of effort. Ludwig bongos are ideal for concert use with finger or stick performance.

	Nickel	Chrome
No. 2358L—Tunable Bongos, choice of lacquer colors.....................	$45.00	$52.00
No. 2358P—Tunable Bongos, choice of pearl colors.....................	52.50	60.00

PART FOUR

THE MUSIC

Single: The Ballad Of John And Yoko / Old Brown Shoe

Released May 30 1969

The Ballad Of John And Yoko

Time Signature - 4/4, 2/4
Recorded - April 14, 1969
Engineer - Geoff Emerick
Drums, Maracas, Handclaps - Paul McCartney
Guitar Body Taps, Handclaps - John Lennon

With Ringo unavailable due to *Magic Christian* filming commitments and George overseas, the impatient John took the opportunity to enlist the enthusiastic Paul to record a new track, destined to be the new Beatles single.

Once again picking up sticks, McCartney delivers an admirable if unspectacular job, busying himself with a repetitive 4/4 beat, with off-beat bass drum adding a welcome variation to the lengthy verses, providing a counterpoint to the vocals.

Perhaps mindful of Ringo's absence, and eager to utilise any object to obtain the sound they had in their minds, Lennon enthusiastically bolsters the snare beat by slapping the back of his acoustic guitar, further enhanced by added handclaps, evident in the left channel of the mix.

A 'cheeky' 2/4 bar with urgent 8th note snare (bar 4 below) punctuates the lyrical 'joke'.

With maracas joining the fray, the otherwise busy mix (the first Beatles stereo UK single release) is nonetheless pleasing on the ear, perhaps due to the laid–back feel of the repetitive beat.

Paul allows himself a break in the steady flow, punctuating the latter stages twice - first on snare -

- then on snare and tom at the point he couldn't resist - preceding the dramatic vocal of the final verse.

Another creditable drumming performance from McCartney, his last for the Beatles - or was it?

Old Brown Shoe

Time Signature - 4/4
Recorded - April 16, 18, 1969
Engineer - Geoff Emerick
Drums - Paul McCartney *or* Ringo Starr
Rim Clicks - Paul McCartney *or* Ringo Starr

Since its release, *Old Brown Shoe* has been regarded as something of a 'hidden gem' amongst Ringo's Beatles performances. However, the release of the *Abbey Road Super Deluxe Edition* in 2019 contained the following 'bombshell' -

*"When The Ballad Of John And Yoko was recorded on Monday 14
April, due to the continuing Magic Christian shooting schedule he was locked into, Ringo did not attend the session. Two days later, he was still unavailable due to filming, so Paul played in his place."*

An enquiry by a Twitter user to remix engineer Sam Okell if this was indeed the case elicited the response - "Yep".

Concerning Ringo's unavailability, why would a recording session that (unusually for the Beatles) began in the afternoon, be scheduled without him? We asked Bill Minto, a veteran of British TV and Film, for his thoughts. *"Shoots would be around 8-10 hours in length, most crews were on a 'buy-out' with time available to complete the schedule if required. If they were shooting at location they couldn't return to, they'd overrun to complete. Night shoots would have been commonplace due to location availability, with the working day starting after lunchtime/mid afternoon. With filming also taking place at Twickenham, even though he was a 30 minute drive away, Ringo could have been unavailable at any time of the day, even when he would have been expected at a Beatles session. Plus, if he was shooting late after a long day and had a 7 or 8 am start the following day, would he really dash across town to drum on a session?"*

Is it possible Ringo could have joined the session later and contributed to Old Brown Shoe? In the *Complete Recording Sessions,* Mark Lewisohn documented overdubs were completed two days later, but with no mention of drums or percussion. However there is clearly at least one percussion overdub - rim clicks are evident on the left channel of the finished track. It is therefore entirely possible there were additional overdubs - quite possibly the signature Ringo snare/tom triplets that are poorly executed on take 2? However, the toms appear to be part of the 'core' drum track. If they were recorded as overdubs they'd surely be on the left channel with the rim clicks? In another twist, Paul is again documented as drumming in the evening session, this time on an unreleased attempt at George's *Something*, so again, no Ringo!

So, if it is indeed Paul drumming, why were we all under the impression it was Ringo? Firstly, contradictory evidence exists concerning the session. Prior to the *Abbey Road Super Deluxe Edition,* in his 1988 book Mark Lewisohn logged Ringo as very much present and drumming on *Old Brown Shoe*. Additionally, Paul has gone on record as stating whilst he is confident in his drumming, he is unable to successfully master a shuffle beat.

With this in mind, *Old Brown Shoe* can be traced back to the *Let It Be/Get Back* sessions earlier in the year, where Ringo utilised the distinctive shuffle that was carried through to the final release. Illustrated here, the simple but effective beat is enhanced by the addition of the overdubbed rim clicks -

Witness the distinctive Ringo style triplet hi-hat/snare combination -

0.19

The middle - 8 section switches to an all-out shuffle, with rim clicks once again emulating the bass drum pattern-

1.04

Replicated again here on snare and floor tom - reminiscent of Ringo's playing as far back as 1964 on *Tell Me Why*, and as evidenced by the scrappy attempts during Take 2 of *Old Brown Shoe*, surely too much for a novice drummer such as McCartney?

1.21

Regardless of the merits of who does or does not drum, *Old Brown Shoe* can still be regarded as a fine drumming performance, one of the Beatles' very best.

LP: Abbey Road

Released September 26 1969

Producer - George Martin
Engineers - Geoff Emerick, Phil McDonald, Jeff Jarratt, Glyn Johns, Tony Clark, Barry Sheffield.

Come Together

Time Signature - 4/4
Recorded - July 21/22/23/25/29/30, 1969
Engineers - *Geoff Emerick, Phil McDonald*
Drums, Maracas - *Ringo Starr*
Handclaps - *John Lennon*

Setting the tone of the album, Ringo's snare and toms have that signature Beatles late-era distinctive sound. Dampened with tea-towels, the resonance of the drums is removed, a counter-point to the bright cymbals and 'fat' sound of the bass drum.

Perhaps the Beatles song most recognisable by the drums alone, *Come Together* features clearly defined and distinctive drum patterns devised by Starr and McCartney.

Leading with his left hand, the distinctive and terrifically quirky introduction sees Ringo performing an incredibly tight yet fluid 'around the kit' movement, from cymbal to hi-hats to toms.

It is worth noting, Ringo rearranged his set up to record Come Together, with his crash/ride cymbal placed between his toms

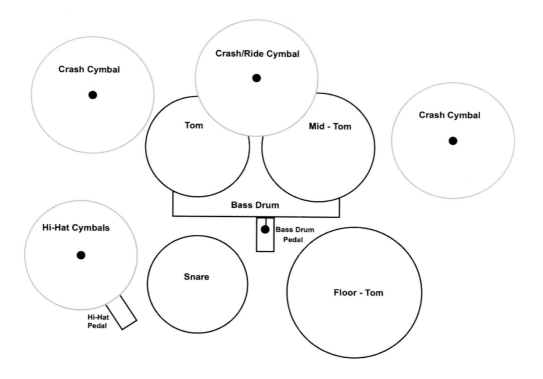

Lennon's exuberant handclaps enhance the first bars, underpinning the album's strong opening.

In a minimalist mood, we hear Ringo bolstering the solidity of the verses with a simple yet effective floor-tom/tom/ bass drum beat, accenting the '1,2,3,4' beats of the bar.

The short bridge between verses has Ringo playing 'dotted' quavers on his bass drum, lending a 'lazy' feel to proceedings, before returning to the song's signature pattern.

0.26

Another minimalist beat this time between snare and bass drum (bars 4 and 5 below), has the effect of 'lengthening' the second bridge, this time falling over the title lyrics.....

1.01

6

.....before settling on a simple yet typically laconic and forceful beat (bar 6 below) during the instrumental break. Hand claps are reintroduced, tentatively added to the mix.

Ludwig Drums

1.47

5

Ludwig Drums

Hand Clap

With the addition of an overdubbed shaker, the play-out bars see Ringo exploring the full expanse of his Hollywood kit, with tom triplets and sextuplets garnishing the move to the fade.

Come Together features a truly fantastic performance from Ringo, disciplined and restrained, while also inventive and expansive. Little wonder the song was chosen as the album opener and is often found at the top of the list of the Beatles streaming charts.

Something

Time Signature - 4/4

Recorded - April 16, May 2/5, July 11/16, August 15, 1969

Engineers - Jeff Jarratt, *Glyn Johns, Phil McDonald*

Drums, Cymbal, Handclaps- *Ringo Starr*

Hi-Hat - *Paul McCartney*

The range of Ringo's playing here is stark - from gentle cymbal strokes to thunderous fills, Ringo plays for the emotion of the song. Taking a cue from the previous track, Ringo brings in the song with overly simplistic tom fills, repeated with slight variations throughout. Overdubbed cymbal, perhaps played with timpani mallets, embellishes the introduction.

Save for the final bars, Starr declines the opportunity to pad the song out with a steady beat. Instead we have a sparse snare and bass beat, with fills appropriately placed between the vocal.

Ringo takes it up a notch during the angst-ridden middle 8 section, with busy and inventive sextuplet tom patterns greatly enhancing George's anguished vocal. Throughout his career Ringo has displayed a strength that belies his diminutive stature - witness his snare/tom work on *Tell Me Why* (1964) and *Help!* (1965). Here, Ringo could have simply played the pattern evenly across two hands, however he sees fit to effortlessly lead with his strong right hand, adding power and purpose to the passage that may otherwise have been lacking.

The song also takes an unusual twist here with the additional hi-hat, surprisingly *not* played by Ringo. While it *is* possible to play the pattern with the hi-hat, it is interesting to note the hi-hat is played by Paul - not as an overdub but in tandem with Ringo.

Giles Martin explains - *"Ringo is playing toms with both hands, and then in the middle bit, Paul goes over to hit the hi-hat, It took the two of them to play drums on that"*.[12]

An unusual arrangement for sure, but again one that perfectly compliments the song. Barely perceptible, Ringo overdubbed handclaps to the already busy percussive arrangement.

Paul's contribution also hints at the composition of this particular drum passage originating from his suggestions, not for the first time a Beatles classic has benefitted from his inventive and creative input. However there is a striking post-script to this suggestion. *Unfaithful Servant* from The Band's self-titled 1969 LP contains the very same hi-hat pattern, albeit at a much slower tempo.

With *The Band* LP not being released until four days prior to *Abbey Road,* it would appear impossible for *Something* or *Come Together* to have been directly influenced by Levon Helm's distinctive playing. However, during a late 1968 visit to the U.S.A George Harrison spent time jamming with Bob Dylan and The Band, where it is quite possible they performed *Unfaithful Servant.* Additionally, due to his enduring friendship with the group, it is entirely plausible he was handed an advance copy of their new LP, which he would surely have circulated amongst his bandmates?

Returning to what we *do* know, the guitar solo features surprising 32nd notes between his mounted toms (1st bar below), the seemingly busy nature of the fill followed by 'dotted' notes that perfectly mimics the phrasing of George's guitar work (bars 4 and 5 below).

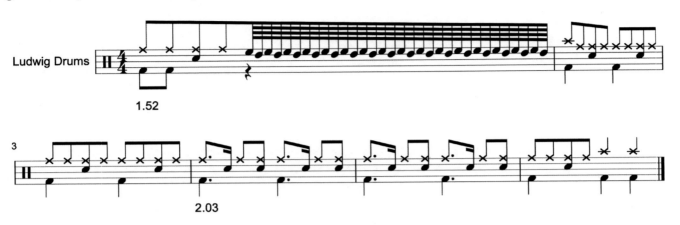

The final bars have Ringo finally settling on a straight hi-hat beat, before 'lifting off' to the finale on bass drum and crash cymbal.

Something is without doubt a fine example of Ringo 'playing for the song'.

Maxwell's Silver Hammer

Time Signature - 4/4

Recorded - July 9/10/11, August 6 1969

Engineers - *Phil McDonald, Tony Clark*

Drums, Anvil - *Ringo Starr*

A McCartney 'leftover' from the *Let It Be* sessions (and not so privately derided by his bandmates), this simplistic yet dark 'nursery crime' sees Ringo plodding along merrily, utilising a bass drum/open and closed hi-hat pedal combination that lends a playful yet sinister feel to the song.

Maxwell's Silver Hammer features quite possibly the Beatles' most bizarre choice of object as a percussion instrument - an anvil. Originally played by Mal Evans on the earlier *Let It Be* sessions version, here Ringo takes up the challenge of lifting the hammer. Note the use of his sizzle cymbal, the long decay of which carries through to the chorus (1st to 5th bars).

Sparing use of bass drum and cymbal, followed by heavily dampened tom and floor tom precede the following verse (last 2 bars above), busier examples outlined below.

Oh! Darling

Time Signature - 12/8

Recorded - April 20/26, July 17/18/22, August 11, 1969

Engineers - Jeff Jarratt, *Phil McDonald, Geoff Emerick,*

Drums - *Ringo Starr*

Classic Ringo - seemingly loosely played, yet employed with precision. Utilising a 'Blues/Doo-Wop' 12/8 meter, Ringo lays down a solid and hi-hat busy beat.

Once again, snare and toms are heavily dampened, lending a simplistic air to the drum track that belies the complexity of Ringo's work here, occasionally at odds with the feel of the track. A slight application of reverb at the mixing stage may have remedied this, an approach somewhat employed by the 2019 remix.

As evidenced by previous takes, Ringo was working within a framework of ideas with regards to his fills, his decision making carried out spontaneously. Here we have sextuplet and triplet fills preceding the middle-eight section.

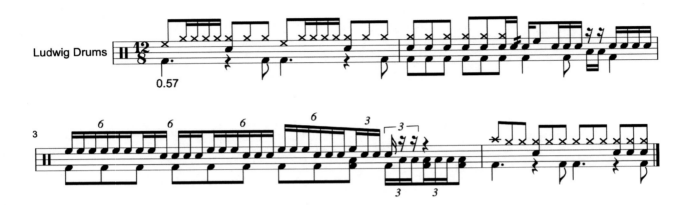

Occasionally playful (bouncing along happily, 3rd bar below), sometimes strong and precise (4th bar), Ringo perfectly captures the emotion of the song, the lack of bounce-back from the tea-towel dampened drums requiring the foresight to strike heavily or otherwise.

Octopus's Garden

Time Signature - 4/4

Recorded - April 26/29, July 17/18, 1969

Engineers - Jeff Jarrett, *Phil McDonald*

Drums, Tom Toms - *Ringo Starr*

Conceived during his brief sojourn from the *White Album* sessions, *Octopus's Garden* is a return to the Ringo album-cameo of old. Possessing the panache and gravitas of being recorded while simultaneously singing and drumming, Ringo punctuates the opening guitar introduction, a simple tom/snare fill leads us to the framework of the song. Ringo's patterns perfectly compliment the simplistic and playful nature of the song.

The instrumental break sees overdubbed toms enhancing the simplistic floor/mid tom work of the backing track.

The final bars see a laconic yet jaunty Ringo ramp up his fills, ending the track as it began.

Simplicity personified, belying a carefully crafted and subtly executed performance.

I Want You (She's So Heavy)

Time Signature - 6/8, 4/4, 2/4

Recorded - February 22, April 18/20, August 8/11, 1969

Engineers - Jeff Jarratt, *Phil McDonald, Geoff Emerick, Barry Sheffield*

Drums, Congas, Wood Blocks - *Ringo Starr*

Topping and tailing the song in 6/8 time, we are soon in familiar Lennon territory – with a short and sparse (compared to the end!) 6/8 introduction, soon followed by 4 bars in 4/4, and in typical Lennon fashion, an additional bar of 2/4 which then takes us into the verse proper. Utilising the bell of his ride cymbal, Ringo punctuates the air with little reserve, setting the tone and direction of the song.

The stop/start nature of the song is smoothed over by the use of open ride and crash/ride cymbals, negotiating the slipping in of a 2/4 bar -

Interruptions come thick and fast, mimicking the anguish of the vocal, another sharp bar of 2/4 containing a stark bass/snare/cymbal triplet, followed swiftly by another punctuation, this time via a snare ruff -

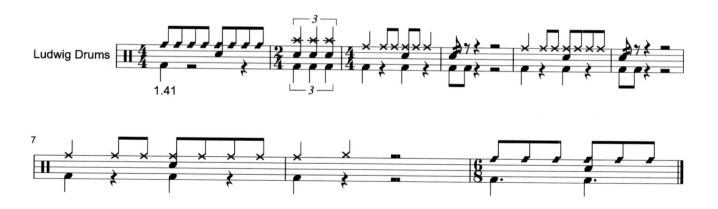

A variation on the bossa-nova beat lends the song a "lounge" feel, due in part to the liberal use of ride cymbal and overdubbed 'free-styling' congas.

The bossa-nova beat returns, this time embellished sparingly by wood blocks -

With plenty of improvisation on the final repetitive passage, especially from multi tracked guitars and the busy bass, Ringo reinforced his drum track, overdubbing snare and tom to bind the performance together. Keeping it simple, power is still present, almost as if his performance has been waiting for the tom roll at [6.26], and when it arrives, it's at just the right moment.

Ringo maintains the frenetic feel, thrashing his way through to the abrupt ending.

Here Comes The Sun

Time Signature - 4/4, 2/4, 3/8, 5/8

Recorded - July 7/8/16, August 6/15/19, 1969

Engineers - *Geoff Emerick, Phil McDonald, Tony Clark*

Drums, Snare, Cymbal, Handclaps - *Ringo Starr*

Handclaps - *George Harrison, Paul McCartney*

"George had been to India, and he says to me "I've got this song, it's like…. '7 & 1/2 time'….he might as well have talked to me in Arabic!. I had to find some way…that I could physically do it, and do it every time, so that it came 'off' on the time. That's one of those Indian tricks, I had no way of going '1,2,3,4,5,6…7' - that's not how my brain works".
Ringo Starr [13]

An excellent example of Ringo's ability to cope with consecutive signatures, *Here Comes The Sun* is also notable for a fantastically laid-back groove. The opening bars set the tone with a delightful double-fill, with bass drum playing around the snare beats.

Subtly mixed overdubbed snare and cymbal bolster the lead to the chorus -

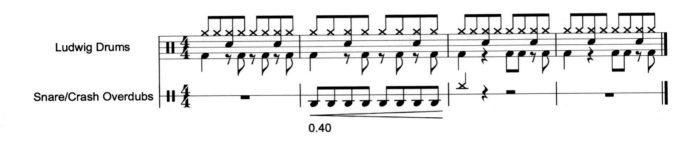

Bridging the chorus to the second verse, Ringo utilises a simple yet effective fill from snare to tom, brightening up the background with the rare use of a splash cymbal (bars 5 and 6) -

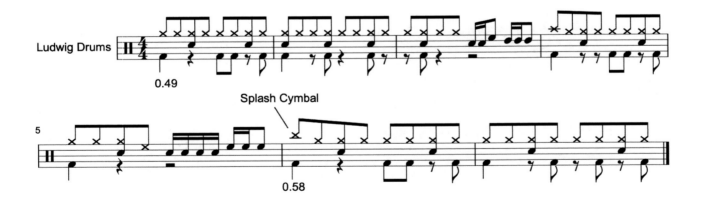

The numerous time changes within the song first occur in the bridge with a bar of 2/4, before alternating between 3/8, 5/8, 4/4, repeating again before returning to 4/4. Here Ringo draws upon his experiences of Indian time-keeping rather than counting out the time in the style of Western music.

1.27

Sharp and snappy handclaps hasten the end of the bridge, cleverly used to great effect. The complexities of three Beatles (George, Paul and Ringo) simultaneously successfully negotiating the minefield of shifting time signatures becomes apparent in the bars below. None of them misses a beat.

Ringo's drums sound fantastic here, benefitting greatly from the new mixing desk and skins. The snare and hi-hats sound crisp and tight, with the drums possessing a punch and weight typical of Geoff Emerick's engineering skills.

Because

Time Signature - 4/4

Recorded - August 1/4/5, 1969

Engineers - *Geoff Emerick, Phil McDonald*

"We didn't have drum machines in those days, so Ringo was our drum machine"
George Martin [14]

No drums or percussion here, although Ringo did serve a purpose - wiped from the final mix he tapped a simple timekeeping beat for the guitarist Beatles while they laid down the backing track.

You Never Give Me Your Money

Time Signature - 4/4

Recorded - May 6, July 1/15/30/31, 1969

Engineers - Glyn Johns, *Geoff Emerick, Phil McDonald*

Drums, Tambourine - *Ringo Starr*

Wind Chimes - *Paul McCartney*

A typical McCartney 'section by section' composition, Ringo's drums are tacit during the melancholic piano intro, appearing as deft open hi-hat touches at the start of the second verse [0.48]. Notated overleaf is the final bar of hi-hat strokes, leading into the hesitant tom-filled band introduction and a fabulously funky 'choked' hi-hat beat. Tumbling fills bridge the vocal lines as Ringo ramps it up with a funky feeling on the bridge, followed by trademark fills between the twin guitar phrasing (bars 5-7).

Note the addition of drumstick tapping, perfectly complimenting Paul's 'wind-up' piano, reinforcing the nostalgic 'vaudevillian' air to the passage.

A gear-change down (1.32) takes us into a straight 4/4 ride cymbal dominated beat, followed by accented bass drum emphasising cymbal crashes.

Notice how Ringo stresses the phonetics of the vocal with forceful bass and snare drums -

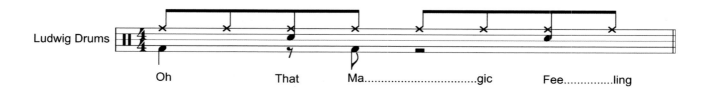

Returning swiftly to the dominant beat, Ringo negotiates a bar of 2/4, then switching to classic Ringo mode - utilising 'dotted' notes to enhance the feel of the song by provide hesitancy (bars 4 and 6 below).

Sparse 'low in the mix' tambourine is introduced, intriguingly either on the final 16th or 8th notes of the bar. Variations on a theme fills punctuate the ensuing lengthy move to the next track, *Sun King*. Wind chimes (played by McCartney) similarly embellish the fade, and are not notated here due being embedded too low in the mix.

Sun King

Time Signature - 4/4

Recorded - July 24/25/29, 1969

Engineers - *Geoff Emerick, Phil McDonald*

Drums, Tambourine, Bongos - *Ringo Starr*

Maracas - *John Lennon*

Utilising timpani sticks, Ringo taps out a measured beat on his tea-towel dampened floor tom while embellishing with deft touches on cymbal. The muted floor tom/cymbal combination mirrors the reverb drenched guitar, adding an exotic sense of mystery to the soundscape. Maintaining the constant, foot pedal hi-hat provides steady timekeeping on the second and fourth beats of the bar (bars six onwards).

Gently played and mixed bongos coupled with gentle maracas enhance the track, the mix a fine example of the EMI staff perfectly complimenting and contributing to the feel of the track.

Sun King was a true group performance, recorded in tandem with the following song *Mean Mr. Mustard.* As evidenced on the *Beatles Rock Band* isolated tracks, Ringo can be heard exchanging timpani mallets for drumsticks - just in the nick of time!

Mean Mr. Mustard

Time Signature - 4/4, 12/8
Recorded - July 24/25/29, 1969
Engineers - *Geoff Emerick, Phil McDonald*
Drums, Tambourine - *Ringo Starr*

After successfully switching to drumsticks and performing a tight opening fill, Ringo settles into a solid groove alongside Paul's languid fuzz bass guitar. This has the effect of adding a cartoon character substance to Mr. Mustard and his odd ways. Not so subtle sixteenth-note tambourine embellishes from the fifth bar onwards, with cymbal slurs bridging bars, as illustrated in the final two bars here -

Resolving the song, Lennon inserts two bars of 12/8 to accommodate the "dirty old man" lyrical phrasing. Note Ringo's final flourish into *Polythene Pam*, with flams from snare to tom.

0.59

Polythene Pam

Time Signature - 4/4

Recorded - July 25/28/30, 1969

Engineers - *Geoff Emerick, Phil McDonald*

Drums, Tambourine, - *Ringo Starr*

Cowbell, Maracas, Handclaps - *Uncredited - listed here as Ringo Starr*

With the apparently impatient Lennon reputably unhappy with the drum track laid down live,[15] Ringo later relaid the recurring tom patterns that became such a feature of this song. Again, it is testament to his overdubbing skills he was able to play over the drum track, perfecting the busy beat as laid out here -

Workmanlike, yet effective and precise, Ringo's tom work (accented and landing with snare on the 4th beat of the bar) keeps the track motoring along.

Making full use of his toms, the fantastically busy percussion track builds progressively, tambourine introduced with cowbell and maracas -

doubling up [1.11] towards the climax with tambourine.

1.09

- leading us into.........

She Came In Through The Bathroom Window

Time Signature - 4/4, 2/4
Recorded - July 25/28/30, 1969
Engineers - *Geoff Emerick, Phil McDonald*
Drums, Tambourine, Slapstick - *Ringo Starr*

Recorded as one track with Polythene Pam, from John's overly Scouse "Oh! Lookout! " followed by Ringo's introductory fill and groove, you know this is going to be a real 'mover'. Filling the void and underpinning the intro is prominent tambourine, with '16 in the bar' hi-hats following, the song moves along at a pace slower than Ringo's playing suggests.

Plentiful, sympathetic fills (the best of which are heard typically 'coming off' the open hi-hat) are bolstered by the reintroduction of tambourine at [0.29].

A bar of 2/4 bridges the verses, providing a welcome respite from the busy hi-hat -

The Beatles were not averse to employing unusual percussion instruments, but here, mimicking the feel of Polythene Pam, we hear an orchestral slap stick landing initially on the '3 and' beats and then adding urgency on the '1 and' beat. An unusual but effective choice, the act of 'slapping' what is essentially conjoined pieces of wood together requires a degree of dexterity. Success is dependant upon the first movement of the slap stick being consistent across the passage of music, and while consistency is evident here, the looseness of the strikes, allied to the natural reverb, adds just the right amount of 'feel' to the song.

Overdubbed tom joins the slap stick, lending a playful air. Notice how Ringo cuts short the tom on the fourth beat, allowing the slap stick more impact.

A fantastically 'musical' performance by Ringo, the smooth beat driving the song, embellished with creative percussion for maximum effect. A real high-point of *Abbey Road,* and indeed Ringo's career.

Golden Slumbers

Time Signature - 4/4

Recorded - July 2/3/4/30/31, August 15, 1969

Engineers - *Geoff Emerick, Phil McDonald*

Drums - *Ringo Starr*

After the lengthy melodic piano introduction, thunderous tom fills, punctuated by bass drum/cymbal crashes, serve to highlight the change in the now searing vocal. Ringo's hitting hard here, extracting maximum volume from his calf skins.

There's plenty of light and shade here, with bars of powerful accents in the chorus, and slight, delicate cymbal strokes enhancing the second verse, joined at [1.20] with the interplay of the tom.

Another forceful fill, virtually identical to that which announced *Golden Slumbers,*

expertly guides us into...

Carry That Weight

Time Signature - 4/4, 2/4

Recorded - July 4/23/30/31, August 15, 1969

Engineers - *Geoff Emerick, Phil McDonald*

Drums, Snare, Floor Tom, Foot Stamps, Timpani[16] **-** *Ringo Starr*

With a prominent drum track evident in the left channel, overdubbed snare, floor tom and foot stamps in the right channel, the result is a heavy drum sound, carrying the weight of the song, so to speak. After a fill that utilises all available drums, Ringo gets his teeth into proceedings from the 'get-go' -

Enhanced by George Martin's orchestral score, Ringo punctuates the reprise of *You Never Give Me Your Money*, before settling down to a no-nonsense beat, allowing the guitar solo space to breathe -

Further punctuation arrives, this time in dramatic fashion, Ringo making way for the ever so clumsy overdubs of foot stamps and drums -

A less disciplined beat follows, with sharp bass drum leading us to a bar which due to a tape edit is best notated here as 2/4, signalling a change in tempo and direction to *The End*.

The End

Time Signature - 4/4

Recorded - July 23, August 5/7/8/15/18, 1969

Engineers - *Geoff Emerick, Phil McDonald*

Drums - *Ringo Starr* [17]

Ringo's showpiece drum solo very nearly didn't happen – dead-set against the idea of a solo, it took a great deal of encouragement from his bandmates (and engineers), plus their agreement to halve the allotted time of the solo, before he would step behind his kit. Ringo's drums on *The End* benefitted from two improvements, namely the fitting of new calf skin heads and the ability for them to be recorded in stereo. Due to the expanded inputs of the TG12345 mixing desk, twelve microphones were apparently utilised in the recording.

The tape edit transition segues from *Carry That Weight* into hard hitting cymbal/snare/bass drum, punctuating 8 in the bar floor tom, bridged by a high and mid tom flourish, perfectly pre-empting Ringo's solo. He's hitting hard here, belying his diminutive stature.

As for the solo itself, it is heavily influenced and inspired by Iron Butterfly's *In-A-Gadda-Da-Vida,* released the previous year. While more expressive and a great deal lighter in approach, drummer Ron Bushy's influence is evident in *The End,* Ringo's emulation of the 8 in the bar bass drum sets the tone, enabling him to concentrate his efforts on his tom work.

Notated here is Ringo's 8 bar drum solo -

Ringo ramps it up towards the guitar solos - with busy bass drum he drives the group forward (bars 5 & 6, 13 & 14 below) - either side of a relatively straight forward but funky-feel beat -

Coming to an abrupt halt, McCartney's heartfelt piano/vocal negotiates time-bending bars of 3/8 before Ringo's forceful toms blast us towards the conclusion. Notice how sparingly utilising the instruments at his disposal, Ringo's restraint heightens the tension and expectation of the final bars.

A fitting end to the album, and indeed, Ringo's performances throughout.

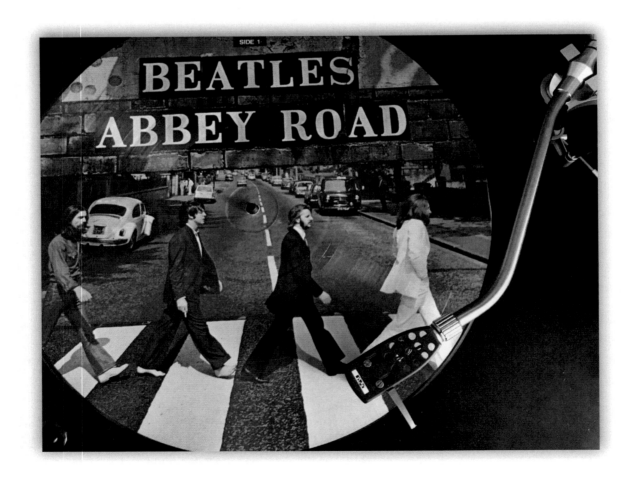

PART FIVE

ABBEY ROAD AND PERCUSSION

Use of Percussion On *Abbey Road*

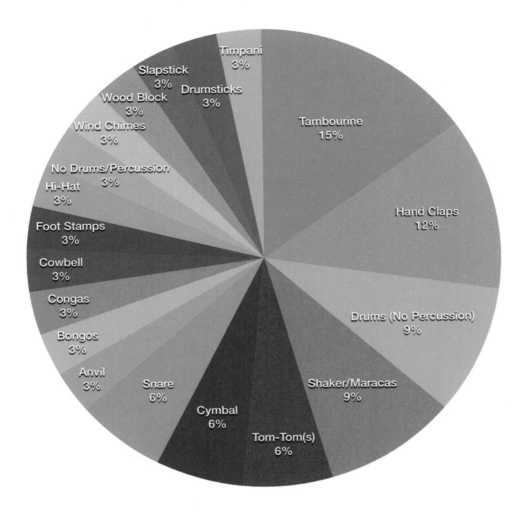

17 Songs

INSTRUMENT	USE
Anvil	1
Bongos	1
Congas	1
Cowbell	1
Foot Stamps	1
Hi-Hat	1
None	1
Wind Chimes	1
Wood Block	1
Slapstick	1
Drumsticks	1
Tom-Tom(s)	2
Cymbal	2
Snare	2
Shaker/Maracas	3
Hand Claps	4
Drums (Solo)	4
Tambourine	5

With the bulk of *Abbey Road* [18] encompassing a less diverse range of musical styles than the Beatles' previous 'complete' LP, the *White Album,* the LP possesses far less exotic percussion choices than its predecessor. This is perhaps in part due to the minimalistic 'back to basics' edict of the *Let It Be* sessions carrying through to *Abbey Road*. Indeed, the most unusual percussive choice, the anvil featuring in *Maxwell's Silver Hammer,* harks back to the *Let It Be* rehearsals. The other surprising choice, while not as unusual, is an orchestral slapstick. Appearing in a Beatles recording for the first time, the slapstick can at least be classed as a traditional instrument, as unusual and striking it may appear to be.

First utilised on *Please Please Me*'s *Do You Want To Know A Secret?,* drum stick tapping makes a welcome return on *You Never Give Me Your Money,* although the intent and effect of the drum sticks is rather different. Otherwise, percussion choice takes us down the 'traditional Beatle' route, with tambourine yet again proving the percussive instrument of choice, closely followed by handclaps and shakers/maracas.

Surprisingly, traditional choices such as bongos and congas feature only once each, while three songs (*Oh! Darling, Golden Slumbers, The End*) feature no percussion, Ringo's drums proving adequate. Only one song (*Because*) features no drums or percussion, although it is worth noting Ringo provided a simple time-keeping beat which was erased from the mix.

Abbey Road Percussion Use By Band Member

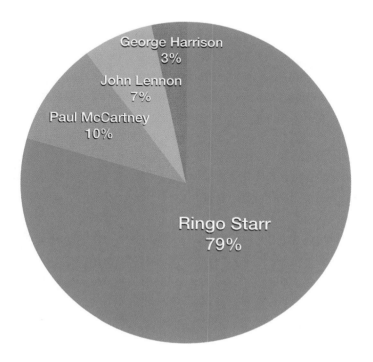

Musician

INSTRUMENT	USE
Ringo Starr	23
Paul McCartney	3
John Lennon	2
George Harrison	1

In addition to the three songs featuring only drums, Ringo as percussionist comes to the fore twenty three times, playing instruments or items as wide-ranging as timpani, anvil, tambourine, foot stomping, congas, drumsticks, and tom toms.

It comes as no surprise that Paul McCartney is the next most prolific percussive Beatle on *Abbey Road*, although this is tempered by the fact he only performs percussion on three songs (*Something, Here Comes The Sun, You Never Give Me Your Money*). As they are considered a percussion instrument, we have included his playing of wind chimes on the latter, although this use lacks true percussive intent.

John Lennon's lack of percussive activity is not unusual when compared to previous Beatles sessions, but can be explained by his recuperation from a motor accident impacting upon his involvement in the *Abbey Road* LP. His sole contribution of handclaps on *Come Together* is lessened by them being performed whilst singing. This reasoning cannot however be attributed to George Harrison, who's handclaps on *Here Comes The Sun* are his sole percussive effort to the album. Previously, George's contributions to Beatles sessions were far more fruitful, with tambourine being his instrument of choice.

It is worth noting that the coda of *Polythene Pam* features maracas, cowbell and tambourine, all officially credited to Ringo Starr as 'percussion'. However, as was the case with previous Beatles sessions, it is highly likely these instruments were played simultaneously by at least three Beatles. As we do not have the precise documentation as to who plays which instrument, we have been guided by the official session documentation of the 50th Anniversary box set book, and credited these instruments to Ringo Starr.

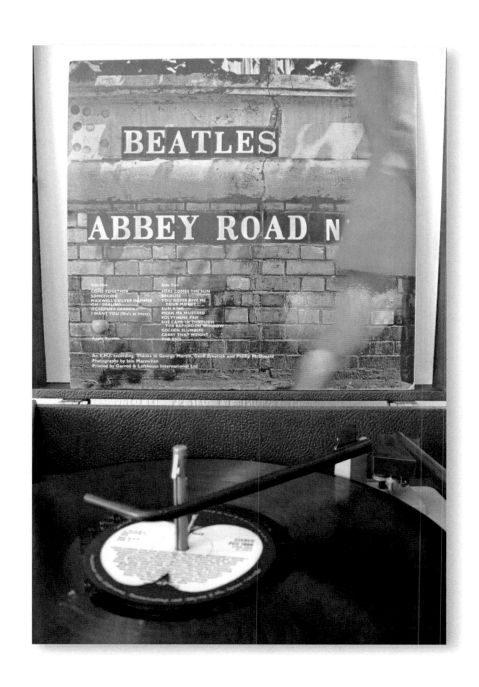

PART SIX

THE SCORES

COME TOGETHER

COME TOGETHER

Transcription © 2020 Alex Cain & Terry McCusker

2

81

3

Fade

4

83

SOMETHING

SOMETHING

Transcription © 2020 Alex Cain & Terry McCusker

2

87

MAXWELL'S SILVER HAMMER

MAXWELL'S SILVER HAMMER

Transcription © 2020 Alex Cain & Terry McCusker

2

91

OH! DARLING

OH! DARLING

Transcription © 2020 Alex Cain and Terry McCusker

2

95

OCTOPUS'S GARDEN

OCTOPUS'S GARDEN

Transcription © 2020 Alex Cain & Terry McCusker

2

99

3

I WANT YOU (SHE'S SO HEAVY)

I WANT YOU (SHE'S SO HEAVY)

Transcription © 2020 Alex Cain & Terry McCusker

2

103

3

4

105

5

106

6

107

HERE COMES THE SUN

HERE COMES THE SUN

Transcription © 2020 Alex Cain & Terry McCusker

2

111

3

YOU NEVER GIVE ME YOUR MONEY

YOU NEVER GIVE ME YOUR MONEY

Transcription © 2020 Alex Cain & Terry McCusker

2

115

SUN KING

SUN KING

Transcription © 2020 Alex Cain and Terry McCusker

sizzle cymbal

2

119

MEAN MR. MUSTARD

MEAN MR. MUSTARD

Transcription © 2020 Alex Cain and Terry McCusker

2

123

POLYTHENE PAM

POLYTHENE PAM

Transcription © 2020 Alex Cain and Terry McCusker

126

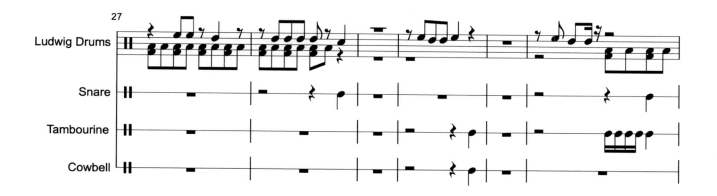

2

127

4

129

SHE CAME IN THROUGH THE BATHROOM WINDOW

SHE CAME IN THROUGH THE BATHROOM WINDOW

Transcription © 2020 Alex Cain and Terry McCusker

2

133

GOLDEN SLUMBERS

GOLDEN SLUMBERS

Transcription © 2020 Alex Cain and Terry McCusker

Ludwig Drums

CARRY THAT WEIGHT

CARRY THAT WEIGHT

Transcription © 2020 Alex Cain and Terry McCusker

2

139

THE END

THE END

Transcription © 2020 Alex Cain and Terry McCusker

HER MAJESTY

Transcription © 2020 Alex Cain and Terry McCusker

16

THE BALLAD OF JOHN AND YOKO

THE BALLAD OF JOHN AND YOKO

Transcription © 2020 Alex Cain and Terry McCusker

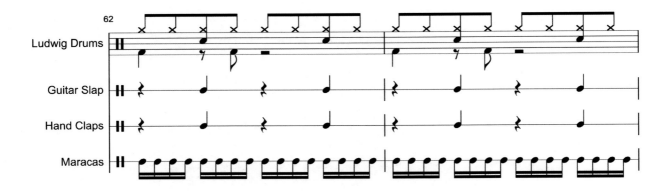

150

4

151

5

7

154

8

155

OLD BROWN SHOE

OLD BROWN SHOE

Transcription © 2020 Alex Cain and Terry McCusker

2

159

© 2020 Alex Cain and Terry McCusker

3

4

161

PART SEVEN

APPENDIX

Acknowledgements

We would like to thank the following individuals for their continued support and encouragement.

Billy Amendola, Gary Astridge, David Bedford, Jerry Hammack, Piers Hemmingson, Freda Kelly, Mark and Carol Lapidos, Mark Lewisohn, Ken Michaels, Bill Minto, Kit O'Toole, Jeff Potter, Anthony Robustelli, Robert Rodriguez, John Rogers, Ben Rowling, Susan Ryan, Al Sussman, Ken Womack.

Many thanks to Daniel Cain for the cover design.

Bibliography

Beatles, T. and Roylance, B. (2000). *The Beatles Anthology*. London: Weidenfeld & Nicolson.

Emerick, G., Massey, H. and Costello, E. (2007). *Here, There and Everywhere: My Life Recording the Music of the Beatles.* New York: Penguin Group (USA).

Lewisohn, M. (1988) *The Complete Beatles Recording Sessions.* Hamlyn.

Womack, K (2019). *Solid State: The Story Of "Abbey Road" and the End of the Beatles*. Cornell University Press.

The Beatles Abbey Road Anniversary Edition (2019). Apple Corps.

Modern Drummer, August 2006

Music Radar, February 2014

Rolling Stone, August 2019

Image Credits

Every effort has been made to correctly acknowledge the source or copyright holder of each illustration and unintentional errors or omissions will be corrected in future editions.

All images © Alex Cain, except -

Page 24 - Josephenus P. Riley / CC BY (https://creativecommons.org/licenses/by/2.0)

Also Available -

From the authors of *Ringo's Abbey Road*

The definitive account of Ringo Starr's drumming with the Beatles

"A beautiful hardback coffee-table book, well-presented over 400-plus pages, with great photos. The stories behind the beats are fascinating and insightful…it's absolutely vital stuff."
***** **Rhythm Magazine**

"A phenomenal reference/entertainment book – everything you want to know about Ringo as a drummer in the Beatles." **Something About The Beatles Podcast**

"There's interesting information here that will get you listening to the Beatles' music in new ways." **Beatlefan magazine**

"Clearly a labor of love……. a smartly compiled Ringo one-stop with an emphasis on the drummer's influential artistry." **Modern Drummer**

www.beatlesbeat.com

Also Available -

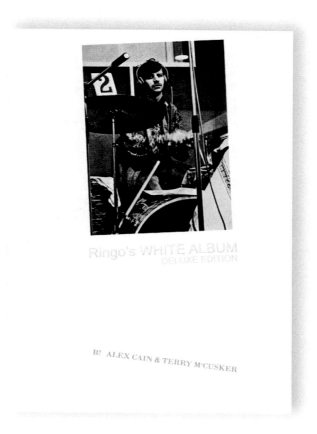

Ringo's White Album

From the authors of *Ringo Starr And The Beatles Beat and Ringo's Abbey Road*, *Ringo's White Album* explores Ringo's contribution to the Beatles' groundbreaking double L.P. *THE BEATLES*, commonly known as the White Album.

Available in two edtions, the Deluxe Edition contains full drum scores of every White Album song (plus the Hey Jude/Revolution single).

"Beatles disciples Alex Cain and Terry McCusker follow up their Ringo Starr And The Beatles Beat with the comprehensive, well researched volume, Ringo's White Album."
Modern Drummer magazine.

www.beatlesbeat.com

Endnotes

[1] *The Beatles Anthology*

[2] Lennon is credited by many sources as appearing on *Carry That Weight,* though the 50th Anniversary box set book does not list him as a performer.

[3] Roy Carr & Tony Tyler in *The Beatles - An Illustrated Record,* quoting Alan Smith of *The New Musical Express*, who famously labelled the *Let It Be* album a 'cheapskate epitaph, a cardboard tombstone'.

[4] Ken Womack - *Solid State - The Story Of Abbey Road And The End Of The Beatles.*

[5] Prime Minister Harold Wilson's 1963 speech warned that if the country was to prosper, a 'new Britain' would have to be forged in the 'white heat' of 'scientific revolution.'

[6] Emerick and Massey, *Here, There, And Everywhere.*

[7] For more information on the Starr Festival snare drum, be sure to check out https://www.starrfestival.info

[8] Session drummer (and good friend of Ringo and George) Jim Keltner has stated Ringo's hi-hat cymbals were 15" in diameter.

[9] *Modern Drummer*, August 2006

[10] *Music Radar* February 2014

[11] *Modern Drummer*, August 2006

[12] Rolling Stone, August 2019

[13] *George Harrison - Living In The Material World*

[14] *The Beatles Abbey Road Anniversary Edition* (2019). Apple Corps.

[15] Geoff Emerick's recollection of Lennon being irritated by Ringo's playing is not borne out by his playful and cheeky comment of Ringo sounding "like Dave Clark".

[16] Ringo has been documented (photographed) as playing timpani on an *Abbey Road* track. If this is the case, it is likely to have been on *Carry That Weight*. However, we have not notated timpani, as it probably co-exists alongside a timpani on George Martin's orchestral score, and as such is indistinguishable in the final mix.

[17] The 50th Anniversary box set book lists Ringo as playing tambourine on *The End,* however we cannot discern this across all versions of the track.

[18] We have not included *Her Majesty* when assessing percussion usage.

ABBEY ROAD

("An E.M.I. Recording")
33⅓
Mfd. in U.K.
SIDE 1

STEREO
PCS 7088
(YEX.749)
℗ 1969

COME TOGETHER (Lennon—McCartney) Northern Songs. NCB.
SOMETHING (Harrison) Harrisongs. MAXWELL'S SILVER
HAMMER (Lennon—McCartney) Northern Songs. NCB.
OH! DARLING (Lennon—McCartney) Northern Songs.
NCB. OCTOPUS'S GARDEN (Starkey) Startling
Music. I WANT YOU (SHE'S SO HEAVY)
(Lennon—McCartney) Northern
Songs. NCB

THE BEATLES
Produced by George Martin

ABBEY ROAD

("An E.M.I. Recording")
33⅓
Mfd. in U.K.
SIDE 2

STEREO
PCS 7088
(YEX.750)
℗ 1969

HERE COMES THE SUN (Harrison) Harrisongs. BECAUSE (Lennon—
McCartney) Northern Songs. NCB. YOU NEVER GIVE ME YOUR
MONEY (Lennon—McCartney) Northern Songs. NCB. SUN
KING (Lennon—McCartney) Northern Songs. NCB. MEAN
MR. MUSTARD (Lennon—McCartney) Northern Songs.
NCB. POLYTHENE PAM (Lennon—McCartney) Northern
Songs. NCB. SHE CAME IN THROUGH THE BATHROOM
WINDOW (Lennon—McCartney) Northern Songs.
NCB. GOLDEN SLUMBERS (Lennon—McCartney)
Northern Songs. NCB. CARRY THAT WEIGHT
(Lennon—McCartney) Northern Songs.
NCB. THE END (Lennon—McCartney)
Northern Songs. NCB

THE BEATLES

Made in the USA
Middletown, DE
03 November 2020